Puzzle, The Brain.

BRAIN EXERCISES

VOLUME 1

BY MESIP

CONTENTS

PREFACE

"Puzzle, The Brain" book contains memory refreshing, and boosting tasks. The variety of tasks included in this volume will help an individual either child or adult to boost their memory power.

Try to solve all the tasks and games in this from Sudoku to Tic Tac Toe without any cheat codes or third-parties.

These puzzles and games need high-quality of thinking capabilities which directly stimulates individual brains.

Let's get into the tasks and stimulate our brain cells with Mathematics.

SUDOKU PUZZLES

Sudoku is a logic-based, combinatorial number-placement puzzle. In classic Sudoku, the objective is to fill a 9 × 9 grid with digits so that each column, each row, and each of the nine 3 × 3 subgrids that compose the grid contain all of the digits from 1 to 9

Sudoku is an excellent brain-stimulating game that any age group can play. As a part of our brain-stimulating exercise, we will solve 4 to 5 sudoku patterns of the 9X9.

- Soduku helps your brain to think, which directly improves your problem-solving skills. So don't cheat yourself in solving the patterns. Think and play.
- As your brain cells work, this game help the brain to remain active.

SUDOKU PUZZLES

PATTERN - 1

							1	
					2			3
			4					
						5		
4		1	6					
		7	1					
	5					2		
				8			4	
	3		9	1				

SUDOKU PUZZLES

PATTERN - 2

								1
							2	3
		4			5			
			1					
				3		6		
		7				5	8	
				6	7			
	1				4			
5	2							

SUDOKU PUZZLES

PATTERN - 3

	9			1			3	
		6		2		7		
			3		4			
2	1						9	8
		2	5		6	4		
	8						1	

SUDOKU PUZZLES

PATTERN - 4

			6		3			
	3			1			5	
		9				2		
7			1		6			9
	2						8	
1			4		9			3
		8				1		
	5			9			7	
			7		4			

SUDOKU PUZZLES

PATTERN - 5

			9		2			
	4						5	
		2				3		
2								7
			4	5	6			
6								9
		7				8		
	3						4	
			2		7			

EIDETIC MEMORY

Eidetic memory is the ability to recall an image from memory with high precision, at least for a brief period of time, after seeing it only once and without using any devices. Eidetic memory refers to the ability to see an object for a few minutes after it is no longer present.

Training Eidetic skills helps people to remember complex things. It's said that chess players train their Eidetic skills to remember complex patterns. Moreover, Eidetic skills can help students and adults in their respective fields to remember the topics and outshine them in their respective fields.

- Try to remember the pictures and their order in the first page and answer the questions in the next page.

EIDETIC MEMORY

TEST - 1

Try to memorize every aspect of these pictures for 2 minutes. And then answer questions on the next page.

EIDETIC MEMORY

TEST - 1

Write down each answer and verify only after answering every question shown below.

- Can you guess the color of the Car?
- How many balls are there at the top of the tennis racquet?
- Name the Kitchen utensils shown there.
- What is placed in the deep left corner?
- How many total pictures are there?
- Is there anything inside the pan?

Don't overturn the page unless you completed the above activity.
If you cannot answer, please try the next test.
On completion, you can move to the next page...

EIDETIC MEMORY

TEST - 2

Try to memorize every aspect of these pictures for 2 minutes. And then answer questions on the next page.

CUP

SNAIL

RUN

GRASS

VOCAL

CLOSE

TOWEL

EIDETIC MEMORY

TEST - 2

Write down each answer and verify only after answering every question shown below.

- Which word is right above the word "CLOSE"?
- Which word has a different color from other words?
- Could you write all six words except the one which is vertically placed?
- Which word is placed right below the word "VOCAL"?
- Name the animal in that picture.

Don't overturn the page unless you completed the above activity.
If you cannot answer, please try the next test.
On completion, you can move to the next page...

EIDETIC MEMORY

TEST - 3

Try to memorize every aspect of these numbers for 2 minutes. And then answer questions on the next page.

7	328
32	8
6	319

EIDETIC MEMORY

TEST - 3

Write down each answer and verify only after answering every question shown below.

- Which is the highest among those numbers?
- Which are the one-digit numbers?
- What is the second digit of two digit number?
- How many three-digit numbers are there?
- What is the third digit of the highest three-digit number?
- How many even numbers are there?

Don't overturn the page unless you completed the above activity.
If you cannot answer, please try the next test.
On completion, you can move to the next page...

EIDETIC MEMORY

TEST - 4

Try to memorize every aspect of these numbers for 2 minutes. And then answer questions on the next page.

EIDETIC MEMORY

TEST - 4

Write down each answer and verify only after answering every question shown below.

- What is the color of fish?
- Name the picture right above the fish?
- How many living things are there in the picture?
- Which continent is shown in earth's picture?
- Name the first picture.
- Which object in that picture is used for transportation?

Don't overturn the page unless you completed the above activity.
If you cannot answer, please try the next test.
On completion, you can move to the next page...

EIDETIC MEMORY

TEST - 5

Try to memorize every aspect of these numbers for 2 minutes. And then answer questions on the next page.

754

1

EIDETIC MEMORY

TEST - 5

Write down each answer and verify only after answering every question shown below.

- What is the third digit in three-digit number?
- Which animal is standing next to number one?
- What is the color of second word in "POOL PARTY"?
- Does the man in the picture has spectac?
- How many black dots are visible on football?

Don't overturn the page unless you completed the above activity.
If you cannot answer, please try the next test.
On completion, you can move to the next page...

LOGICAL PUZZLES

Try to answer the below Logical Puzzle Questions.

Q) Five people were eating apples, A finished before B, but behind C. D finished before E, but behind B. What was the finishing order?

Q) Jack is looking at Anne. Anne is looking at George. Jack is married, George is not, and we don't know if Anne is married. Is a married person looking at an unmarried person?

Q) If five cats can catch five mice in five minutes, how long will it take one cat to catch one mouse?

LOGICAL PUZZLES

Try to answer the below Logical Puzzle Questions.

Q) This conundrum, a variation on a lying/truth problem, has famously been called the hardest logic puzzle ever. You meet three gods on a mountaintop. One always tells the truth, one always lies, and one tells the truth or lies randomly. We can call them Truth, False, and Random. They understand English but answer in their language, with ja or da for yes and no—but you don't know which is which. You can ask three questions to any of the gods (and you can ask the same god more than one question), and they will answer with ja or da. What three questions do you ask to figure out who's who?

LOGICAL PUZZLES

Try to answer the below Logical Puzzle Questions.

Q) There are three people (Alex, Ben and Cody), one of whom is a knight, one a knave, and one a spy. The knight always tells the truth, the knave always lies, and the spy can either lie or tell the truth. Alex says: "Cody is a knave." Ben says: "Alex is a knight." Cody says: "I am the spy." Who is the knight, who the knave, and who the spy?

LOGICAL PUZZLES

Try to answer the below Logical Puzzle Questions.

Q) A farmer wants to cross a river and take with him a wolf, a goat, and a cabbage. He has a boat, but it can only fit himself plus either the wolf, the goat, or the cabbage. If the wolf and the goat are alone on one shore, the wolf will eat the goat. If the goat and the cabbage are alone on the shore, the goat will eat the cabbage. How can the farmer bring the wolf, the goat, and the cabbage across the river without anything being eaten?

LOGICAL PUZZLES

Try to answer the below Logical Puzzle Questions.

Q) The day before two days after the day before tomorrow is Saturday. What day is it today?

Q) You're at a fork in the road in which one direction leads to the City of Lies (where everyone always lies) and the other to the City of Truth (where everyone always tells the truth). There's a person at the fork who lives in one of the cities, but you're not sure which one. What question could you ask the person to find out which road leads to the City of Truth?

WORD LADDER

A word ladder puzzle begins with two words, and to solve the puzzle one must find a chain of other words to link the two, in which two adjacent words (that is, words in successive steps) differ by one letter.

Example,

HEAD - HEAL - TEAL - TELL - TALL - TAIL

Solve,

SAME - - COST

WINE - - BEER

WORD LADDER

Solve,

SAME -	- COST
SLOW -	- DOWN
BATH -	- TUBS
WARM -	- COLD
CAT -	- DOG
BACK -	- FIRE

WORDS WITHIN A WORD

From a single long word try to find out and write as many words as possible.

Word : "example"

Word : "onomatopoeia"

WORDS WITHIN A WORD

Word : "championship"

Word : "microscope"

Word : "gamechanger"

WORDS WITHIN A WORD

Word : "gameover"

Word : "cricket"

Word : "counterparts"

WORDS WITHIN A WORD

Word : "economy"

Word : "rehabilitation"

Word : "brilliant"

WORDS WITHIN A WORD

Word : "sources"

Word : "metropolitan"

Word : "methodology"

SCHULTE TABLE

A Schulte table is a grid with randomly distributed numbers or letters used for development of speed reading, peripheral vision, attention and visual perception.

From the table below, try to find the numbers from 1 to 25 in ascending order as fast as you can with the help of a timer.

6	8	22	1	13
3	4	16	23	15
10	2	18	9	21
25	11	19	20	17
14	24	5	7	12

SCHULTE TABLE

10	2	18	9	21
14	24	5	7	12
6	8	22	1	13
3	4	16	23	15
25	11	19	20	17

As you try to do different charts, improve the timing. This exercise helps your brain to improve your peripheral vision, attention, and memory.

SCHULTE TABLE

Try to improve this skill as possible as you can.

11	4	6	8	16
5	20	1	22	17
3	23	10	15	25
7	19	13	18	24
14	12	9	21	2

SCHULTE TABLE

It is also used to develop attention and concentration.

21	4	7	8	14
2	24	1	22	17
3	23	10	13	25
6	19	15	18	20
16	12	9	11	5

SCHULTE TABLE

25	4	7	6	14
5	19	1	23	18
3	22	10	13	16
8	24	15	17	20
21	12	9	11	2

CROSSWORDS PUZZLES

The goal is to fill the white squares with letters, forming words or phrases that cross each other, by solving clues which lead to the answers. In languages that are written left-to-right, the answer words and phrases are placed in the grid from left to right ("across") and from top to bottom ("down").

1	2	3	4	5
6				
7				
8				
9				■

CROSSWORDS PUZZLES

Hints:
ACROSS
1) "Yabba______doo!"
6) Turn of phrase
7) Transformer scratch pioneer and hip-hop producer DJ ___ Jeff
8) Sweet sandwiches
9) Badminton barriers

DOWN
1) Mustard choice
2) "Not on ___!" ("Ain't happening!")
3) "Carmen" composer
4) Buffoons
5) Adams and Schumer

CROSSWORDS PUZZLES

CROSSWORDS PUZZLES

Hints:
ACROSS
2) Another word for beautiful.
3) Examples of _________ includes donuts, cupcakes, and pudding.
5) Bugs can be _________ if they keeps flying around you.
7) Artists have good imagination and are usually very _________.
8) If a person is ________, they do not get afraid easily.

DOWN
1) If a book or movie teaches you something, it is ________.
4) Something is ________ if it is difficult, hard to understand.
5) Something is ________ when it is really bad.
6) Before you take a difficult rest, you have to ________ for it.

CROSSWORDS PUZZLES

CROSSWORDS PUZZLES

Hints:
ACROSS
2) Mathematical expression where letters are used to represent a value.
4) A letter that represents an unknown value.
5) A fact or rule with Mathematical symbols.
7) A Mathematical statement that shows two Mathematical expressions are equal.
8) A specified term.

DOWN:
1) A Mathematical amount of something.
2) Where letters are used to represent numbers in Mathematics.
3) A value of a number that doesn't change.
4) A symbol of the Alphabet.

CROSSWORDS PUZZLES

Hints:
Reference: "Mistory on Mangolia Circle"

CROSSWORDS PUZZLES

ACROSS
3) The main character of the story.
4) Traits Descriptive adjectives that tell the reader the specific qualities of a character.
8) Joplin The famous pianist who inspired Ivy's dad to get a piano.
11) A person who travels from place to place.
12) The gift Teddy got for his birthday.
14) The inferred moral, message, or lesson of the story.
17) Ivy' best friend.
18) The person Ivy had to wrote an apology letter to.
20) To deny or contradict a statement or accusation.
22) Who looked like "a distinguished professor in serious need of a haircut ."
23) Clues Hints the author gives to help a reader understand a difficult or unusual word.

CROSSWORDS PUZZLES

24) The name of the app Teddy and Ivy used to get rides around city.
26) A street or passage that is closed at one end

DOWN:
1) Showing dignity or authority in one's appearance or manner.
2) Extremely evil, cruel, or wicked.
5) What the story is mostly about. (1 sentence summary)
6) Resistance expressed in action or argument.
7) Showing that you do not think someone or something is worth thinking about or considering.
9) To make a well informed guess.
10) Mission The homeless shelter Melvin Moss was found at.
13) The new mom who was named after winning the lottery.
15) To suffer something difficult, unpleasant, or painful.
16) The cardiologist who loves making waffles.

CROSSWORDS PUZZLES

18) The person that busted Ivy and Teddy for spying on Mr. Hobart.
19) The person who helped Melvin get right with the law.
21) Having both happy and sad characteristics.
25) The mastermind behind the "Torjan War" inspired burglaries.

CROSSWORD PUZZLES

Hints:

ACROSS

1) Spelman or Morehouse, for short

5) Fluffy scarves

9) "Surely, you __!"

13) List-ending abbr.

CROSSWORDS PUZZLES

14) Texter's "What's up?"
15) Black-and-white cookie
16) Denomination of most of the world's Muslims
18) Genesis twin
19) Zesty flavor
20) Saloon
22) "GMA" TV network
23) Teacup pig, e.g.
25) Spiced cold drink made with sweetened condensed milk
29) "Dracula" novelist Stoker
31) Doc intended to protect confidentiality
32) Eggs purchase
33) Spicy pizza topping
36) Clumsy oaf
37) Pro on the slopes
41) __-mo replay
42) Host, as guests
44) Divided Asian peninsula
47) Nape tickler
48) Sharp cry
49) Coastal resort town southeast of Naples

53) __ de plume
54) TiVo button
55) Normal: Abbr.
56) "Silly me!"
58) Brewpub options
60) Nonverbal communication concern, and a phonetic hint to a feature of 16-, 25-, 37-, and 49-Across
65) U. of Maryland athlete
66) Disney warrior played by Liu Yifei
67) Some
68) Online artisan marketplace
69) Dalmatian mark
70) Actress Ward

CROSSWORDS PUZZLES

DOWN
1) "__ So Shy"
2) AC meas.
3) "No time to chat!"
4) Forearm bone
5) Fenway team: Abbr.
6) Duo, the Duolingo mascot, for one
7) Saudi __
8) Poison shrub
9) mActor Pesci
10) Not genuine
11) "We build, we fight" military member
12) Big-billed bird
14) Low's opposite
17) Loan payment pt.
21) Decrease
23) Kid-friendly sandwich, informally
24) History chapters
26) Actresses Sothern and Jillian
27) "Very relatable"
28) Nylabone, e.g.
30) "The Marvelous Mrs. __"
34) Rice dishes

CROSSWORDS PUZZLES

35) Experimental musician Brian
36) Hon
38) Music featuring sitars
39) Like Pyrex
40) Work-related move, for short
43) LP's 33 1/3
44) Discipline taught by a sensei
45) Filled and folded brunch order
46) Indy 500 entrants
47) Prepare for company, in a way
50) Things
51) Minnesota's state bird
52) Hither and __
57) School support orgs.
59) Undercover agent
61) Jeff Lynne's band, informally
62) Feline
63) Cartoon frame
64) Defunct airline

CALCUDOKU PUZZLES

CalcuDoku are math based puzzles coupled with logic. Unlike other logic puzzles, CalcuDoku uses addition, subtraction, multiplication and division in ways which are deeper and more gratifying than anyone can imagine.

CalcuDoku puzzles come in many sizes and range from very easy to extremely difficult taking anything from five minutes to several hours to solve. However, make one mistake and you'll find yourself stuck later on as you get closer to the solution.

Each puzzle consists of a grid containing blocks surrounded by bold lines. The object is to fill all empty squares so that the numbers 1 to N (where N is the number of rows or columns in the grid) appear exactly once in each row and column and the numbers in each block produce the result. In CalcuDoku a number may be used more than once in the same block.

Example:

4×	11+		
	18×		8+
		4×	
2÷			

Puzzle

Solution

4× 1	11+ 4	3	2
4	18× 3	2	8+ 1
3	2	4× 1	4
2÷ 2	1	4	3

CALCUDOKU PUZZLES

9 +		1	5 +
8 +		5 +	
	1 -		2
		1 -	

1 -	4 +		2 -
	1 -	1	
3 -		2 -	2 -
	2		

CALCUDOKU PUZZLES

1 -		3 -	
4	3 -	3 +	5 +
2 -			
	9 +		

7 +	3 -		9 +
	1	8 +	
3	7 +		

CALCUDOKU PUZZLES

9 +	2 -	5 +	4 +	
				2 -
1 -	1 -		2 -	
	1	5 +		3
5 +			1 -	

CALCUDOKU PUZZLES

10 +		10 +	2	4 +
5 +				
	5 +		9 +	
9 +		4 +		7 +
3 +		7 +		

CALCUDOKU PUZZLES

4 +	2 -	5	3 -	
		3 -		2 -
6 +	1 -		2 -	
	4 -			6 +
4 -		1 -		

CALCUDOKU PUZZLES

4	3 -		3 +	12 +
6 +	4 +			
	12 +	1 -		
		3 -		1 -
2	12 +			

CALCUDOKU PUZZLES

3 +	4	12 +	4 -		6 +
			3 -		
4	5 -		2 -		8 +
1 -	1 -		1 -	1	
	3 +			6 +	1 -
3 -		6 +			

CALCUDOKU PUZZLES

3	19 +			6 +	
4 -		2 -		5 -	
3 +	6		3		9 +
	1 -		1 -		
3 -		4 -	3 +	2 -	
1 -				3 -	

CALCUDOKU PUZZLES

3 -		11 +		3 -	2
6 +		13 +			7 +
6			2 -		
10 +	3 -		1 -	1 -	
	5 -	1 -		4 -	
			2 -		6

CALCUDOKU PUZZLES

8 +		3 -		3 -	6
8 +	2 -		2		3 -
	3 -	6	1 -		
4		4 -		9 +	
2 -	2 -	15 +	6 +		3 -

CALCUDOKU PUZZLES

13 +	4 -		7 +		15 +	6 -
	3	3 +	1 -	3 -		
9 +						
5 -		3 -	4 -		10 +	
3	11 +		4	1 -	13 +	5
3 -			6 +			1 -
	1 -					

CALCUDOKU PUZZLES

9 +		4 -	13 +		1 -	
10 +			4 -	19 +		1
5 +	5 -			5		4 -
	2 -	7 +	6 +			
2			2 -		1 -	
3	14 +	3 +		3 -		1 -
		12 +		2 -		

CALCUDOKU PUZZLES

1 -		5 +	12 +	4 +	5 +	3 -
5 -	3 -					
		9 +	6 +		4 -	
2 -	4		13 +		1 -	1 -
	10 +		1	1 -		
10 +		6 +			1	11 +
6 -		2 -		2 -		

TIC-TAC-TOE

Tic-tac-toe, noughts and crosses, or Xs and Os is a paper-and-pencil game for two players who take turns marking the spaces in a three-by-three grid with X or O. The player who succeeds in placing three of their marks in a horizontal, vertical, or diagonal row is the winner

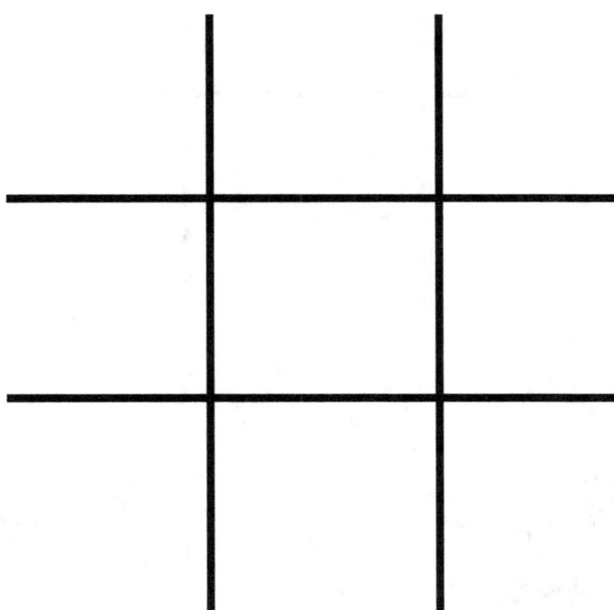

TIC-TAC-TOE

X O

TIC-TAC-TOE

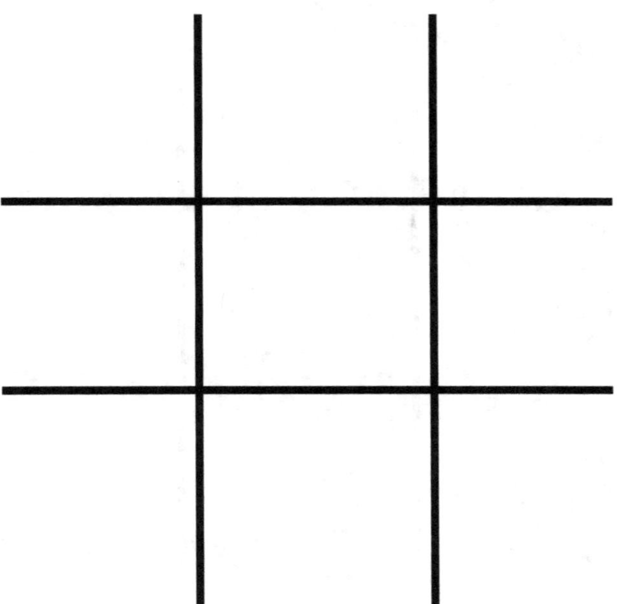

TIC-TAC-TOE

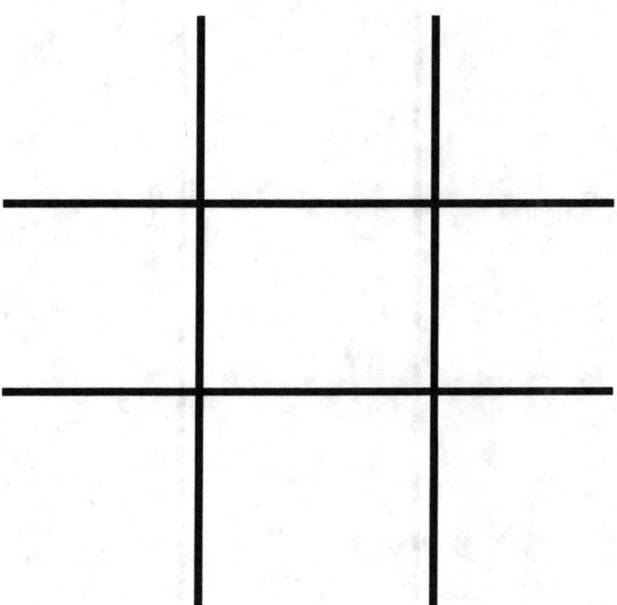

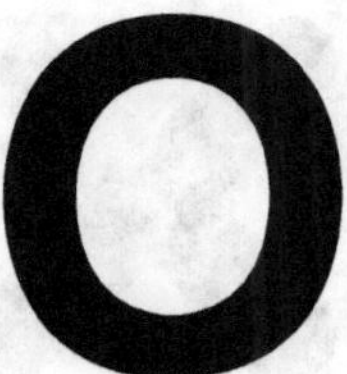

TIC-TAC-TOE

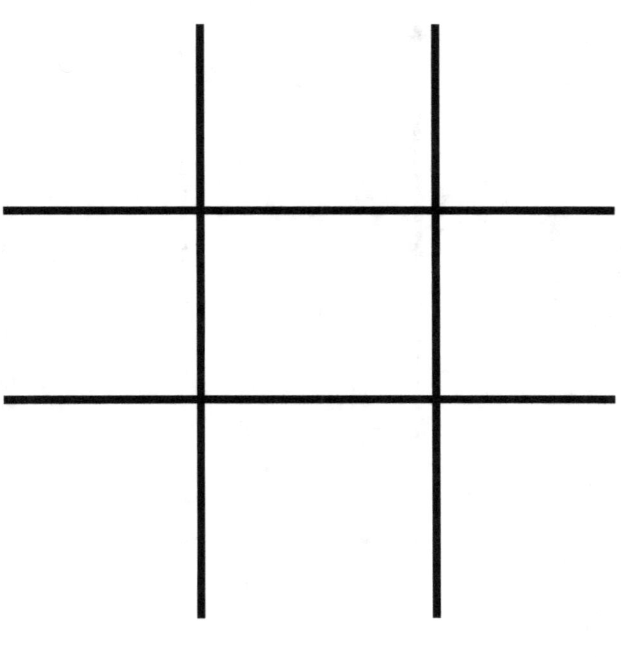

TIC-TAC-TOE

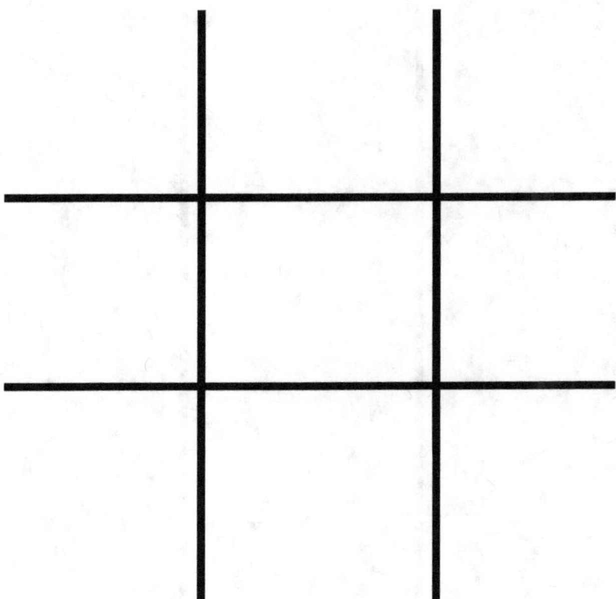

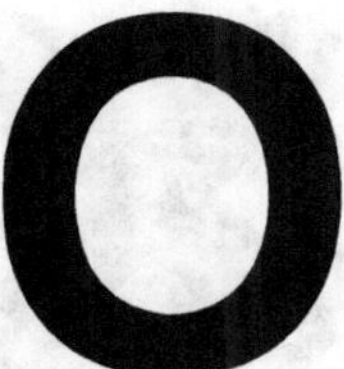

TIC-TAC-TOE

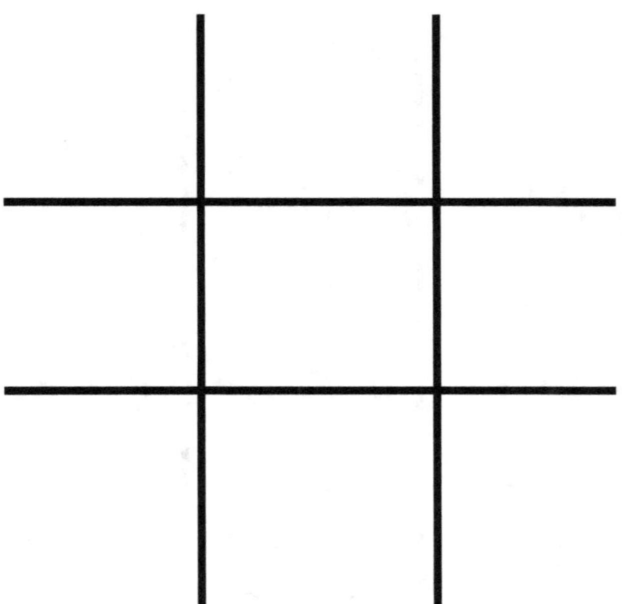

TIC-TAC-TOE

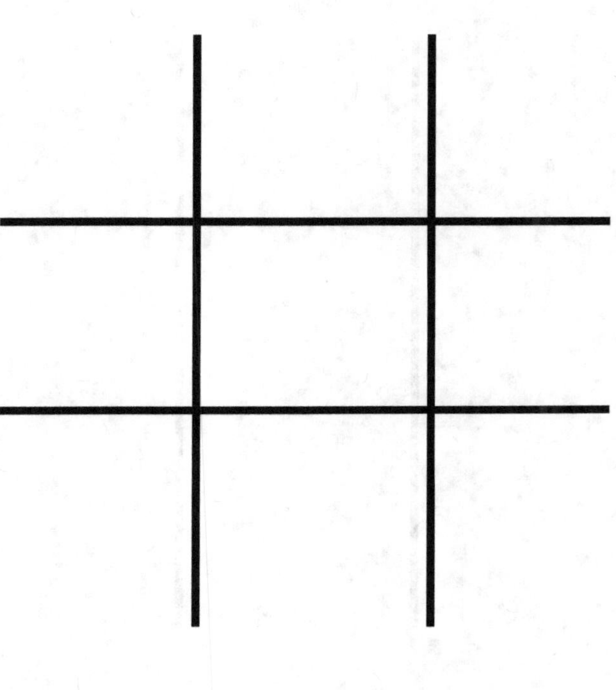

BRAIN EXERCISES

JIGSAW PUZZLE

A jigsaw puzzle is a tiling puzzle that requires the assembly of often irregularly shaped interlocking and mosaiced pieces, each of which typically has a portion of a picture. When assembled, the puzzle pieces produce a complete picture.

Working on jigsaw puzzle is an excellent way to strengthen your brain. Doing jigsaw puzzles recruits multiple cognitive abilities and is a protective factor for visuospatial cognitive aging.

www.ingramcontent.com/pod-product-compliance
Lightning Source LLC
Chambersburg PA
CBHW070957250726
48663CB00002B/270

* 9 7 9 8 8 5 6 7 5 8 3 4 3 *